MW00358893

# 50

## Amazing Cocktails

### Inspired by

# Harry Potter

ARCHIE THOMAS

Published in 2016 by
**Acorn Books**
www.acornbooks.co.uk

Acorn Books is an imprint of
**Andrews UK Limited**
www.andrewsuk.com

Copyright © 2016 Archie Thomas

The right of Archie Thomas to be identified as the author of
this work has been asserted in accordance with the Copyright,
Designs and Patents Act 1998

All rights reserved. No part of this publication may be
reproduced, stored in any retrieval system or transmitted in any
form or by any means, electronic, mechanical, photocopying,
recording or otherwise, without the prior written permission of
the copyright holder for which application should be addressed
in the first instance to the publishers. No liability shall be
attached to the author, the copyright holder or the publishers for
loss or damage of any nature suffered as a result of the reliance
on the reproduction of any of the contents of this publication or
any errors or omissions in the contents.

This book benefits from fair use provisions as set out in
applicable copyright and trademark law. All characters and
relevant information from within the world of Harry Potter are
the intellectual property of J.K. Rowling, to whom all of us are
indebted for bringing us such a wonderful and magical world.

# Contents

*This book is written for all the Harry Potter fans out there who – like me – absolutely love the wizarding world created by JK Rowling. Nothing within this book would have been possible without the incredible stories she wrote for us all – so thank you Jo, from the bottom of my heart!*

# Introduction

Before we get to the cocktails, here's a few thoughts and pieces of advice that are worth bearing in mind if you're thinking of holding a cocktail party – or just want to try out the various recipes within this book.

Firstly, the key to any successful cocktail night is variety – and that means having plenty of ingredients. In addition to the normal spirits such as vodka, whisky (or whiskey, although in this book I've stuck to the former so as not to complicate matters), white rum and gin, you're also going to need a few drinks and accessories that you might not already own, but are still fairly easy to pick up. I've chosen to use Midori (a melon liqueur) for most of the green recipes in this book as it enables you to make cocktails of the most wonderful colour; although it's not a fixture in your average drinks cabinet, it isn't too hard to get hold of. Another is Angustora bitters; you might not know the name but you'll probably recognise the bottle – it's the small one with paper wrapped around it that you've always wondered about! Sugar syrup and Grenadine are both found in the spirits section of most supermarkets and are thankfully not too expensive, and the same can be said for curacao and triple sec. Aside from the bottles, you should also stock up on fresh juices (orange, cranberry and pineapple are the most common), bottled juices (mostly lemon and lime) and fresh fruit – limes, lemons and oranges unsurprisingly. Mint leaves are sometimes used, and you'll probably want to buy a great big bag of ice, as you'll be using plenty of it! Lastly, a jar of cocktail cherries and a bag of specially prepared olives will mean you can add that finishing touch to a drink.

You'll also need a cocktail shaker – it's not just for show, as you'll need to mix and strain plenty of the drinks within this book. A cocktail spoon is handy but not essential (it is a good size to help with the layering of shots) as is a 'muddler' to help you crush mint leaves and suchlike. Investing in some decent glasses is not essential, but can make all the difference to the 'feel' of a drink – a cocktail that should be served in a martini glass just doesn't look right in an old tumbler. You've probably got a potato peeler somewhere handy, which is perfect for creating long slices of orange and lemon peel (curl the peel round a spoon handle to get it into shape after cutting) and having some kind of measuring device around will help you find the right ratio of ingredients.

Lastly, it should be said that whilst making these cocktails can be great fun, you should always drink responsibly and in moderation.

Enjoy the cocktails!
Archie Thomas

# The Cocktails

# Gryffindor

# Godric's Gobbler

Gryffindor's house cocktail is one for the brave. With a (fire) whisky base it's sure to warm you up after a cold evening's quidditch practice...

*Glass: Collins*

- ◆  2 parts whisky
- ◆  1 part brandy
- ◆  1 part cranberry juice
- ◆  2 parts champagne
- ◆  2 lemon slices
- ◆  Ice

➤ Fill a glass half way with ice

➤ Add all the liquids to the glass, then stir lightly

➤ Add one slice of lemon to the drink itself, and another over the glass

➤ Serve

2

# Hufflepuff
## Huff n' Puff

- ◆ 2 parts Midori
- ◆ Orange juice
- ◆ Slice of orange
- ◆ Ice

➤ Add ice to fill the glass three quarters full

➤ Pour in the Midori

➤ Top up with orange juice

➤ Stir – not too much, but enough to blend the two drinks

➤ Add the orange slice to the edge of the glass, ensuring some is placed under the surface of the drink

➤ Serve

*Glass: Wine*

*A nice fruity cocktail to suit almost all tastes, the huff n' puff is easy to make and easy to enjoy. Drink up!*

3

# Ravenclaw

## Blue Lagoon

A smart choice, but drink too much of Ravenclaw's tasty cocktail and you might struggle to solve the eagle knocker's riddle...

- ◆ 2 parts vodka
- ◆ 1 part Blue Curacao
- ◆ 1 dash lemon juice
- ◆ Water
- ◆ Sugar
- ◆ Jelly candy
- ◆ Ice

*Glass: Martini or Collins*

➤ Add the vodka, curacao, lemon juice and ice to a cocktail shaker.

➤ Add enough water to fill your glass then shake well – a martini glass will give a stronger cocktail, whereas a collins is lighter but still just as tasty

➤ Wet the upper rim of your glass, then dip in sugar

➤ Carefully strain the contents of the shaker into the glass

➤ Put the jelly candy on a cocktail stick and rest again the rim. Add a straw then serve

# Slytherin

## Snake Venom

Slytherin's house cocktail may appear to be sweet at first, but don't let that fool you — it's actually got quite a kick and can catch you unawares...

- ◆ 4 parts Midori
- ◆ 1 part lemon juice
- ◆ 1 dash of sugar syrup
- ◆ Cocktail cherry
- ◆ Ice

*Glass: Martini*

➤ Put plenty of ice into a cocktail shaker and add the Midori, lemon juice and sugar syrup – don't use more than a small dash of syrup, it doesn't need much.

➤ Give it a good shake

➤ Pour into the glass and add the cherry on the side.

➤ Serve

5

# Harry Potter

## Classic Mojito

We think Harry would choose this classic; something not too simple, but not too much fuss either. The perfect drink to relax with after saving the world a few times...

*Glass: Collins*

- 2 parts white rum
- ¾ part sugar syrup
- 1 part lime juice
- 3 parts soda water
- A few mint leaves
- Slice of lime
- Ice

➤ Add the sugar syrup and the mint leaves to the glass

➤ Pour in the lime juice then crush the mint leaves well

➤ Fill the glass ¾ full with crushed ice

➤ Pour in the rum, fill with soda and stir gently

➤ Garnish with mint, lime slice and serve

# Minerva McGonagall
## Bloody Mary

Making the perfect Bloody Mary is harder than transfiguration. But some people will settle for nothing else. An interesting drink that is much tastier than you might first think...

- 2 parts vodka
- A couple of dashes of Worcestershire sauce
- 4 parts tomato juice
- ½ part lemon juice
- A pinch of salt
- A dash of tabasco sauce
- Pepper
- Celery
- Slice of lime
- Ice

*Glass: Collins*

➢ Coat the rim of a glass with pepper soaked in Worcestershire sauce

➢ Fill the glass ½ full with ice

➢ Add in the lemon juice and vodka and stir

➢ Now add the salt, a pinch of pepper, tabasco and Worcestershire sauce

➢ Add the tomato juice and stir

➢ Garnish with celery and a small slice of lime then serve

7

# Arthur Weasley
## Ginger Guzzler

This is a really fresh-tasting cocktail that is great for sipping whilst relaxing at the burrow, reading the latest edition of 'Plugs and Fuses Monthly'.

- ◆ 2 parts brandy
- ◆ 6 parts ginger ale
- ◆ 1 dash of angostura bitters
- ◆ Ice

➤ Put plenty of ice into the glass

➤ Pour in the brandy and then the ginger ale

➤ Stir well, *then* add the bitters

➤ Serve

*Glass: Collins*

# Lord Voldemort

# Avada Kedavra

This is the kind of potion only dark wizards should attempt. Like polyjuice it isn't particularly nice, but a few of these and you'll feel like your soul has been split a few times...

- 1 ½ parts whisky
- 1 ½ parts white rum
- 1 ½ parts gin
- 1 ½ parts brandy
- 6 parts stout
- 4 parts champagne
- Ice

→ Half fill a cocktail shaker with ice

→ Add the gin, rum, whisky and brandy to the shaker

→ Shake well then strain into a glass

→ Pour in the stout and stir gently

→ Finally, carefully pour in the champagne and serve

Glass: Long

# Argus Filch
# Secret Squib

Traditionally this is called a 'Long Island Iced Tea'. Depending on how much cola you add to this drink, it will either look like iced tea or simply pure cola. Either way, no-one else will know your secret. Probably...

- ½ part gin
- 1 part white rum
- ½ part tequila
- ½ part Triple Sec
- ½ part vodka
- 1 part sugar syrup
- 1 part lemon juice
- Cola to taste
- Lemon slices
- Ice

*Glass: Fancy*

→ Fill the glass with ice
→ Add in everything but the cola
→ Stir, then add cola to taste
→ Throw in some lemon slices and serve

10

# Peter Pettigrew
## Mudbloody Water

When you're as pathetic as Peter Pettigrew, you'll drink what the Dark Lord tells you to. Muggles call this simply 'Muddy Water' but then what do those idiots know, right?

Glass: Collins

- 2 parts white rum
- 2 parts orange juice
- Cola
- Ice

↣ Fill the glass half full with ice

↣ Pour in the rum and orange juice

↣ Fill with cola and stir gently

↣ Serve

# Sirius Black

## Whisky Sour

It's no surprise that Sirius Black's cocktail would be built upon whisky; this is a classic recipe that has been served for many years...

- 2 parts high quality bourbon
- 1 part lemon juice
- 1 part sugar syrup
- Cocktail cherry
- Lemon slice
- Ice

➤ Add all but the lemon slice and cocktail cherry into a cocktail shaker

➤ Shake well then strain into a short glass

➤ Drop in the cherry and lemon slice; add a cube of ice if required

➤ Serve

*Glass: Rocks*

# Albus Dumbledore

## Dumbledore's Old Fashioned

Yes, we know he is! Very funny. This is another all-time classic cocktail that has been made by generations of bartenders and is traditionally served before dinner.

- 2 parts whisky
- Large dash of Angustora bitters
- Soda water
- Teaspoon of sugar
- Cocktail cherry
- Orange peel
- Ice

→ Add the sugar to the glass then pour in the soda water and the Angustora bitters

→ Stir the ingredients then add ice

→ *After* stirring, pour in the whisky

→ Drop in the cocktail cherry and the orange peel

→ Serve

*Glass: Old Fashioned*

13

# Lucius Malfoy

## Death Eater

- Put some ice into a cocktail shaker

- Add in the whisky, sugar syrup and lime juice

- Slowly add the Grenadine until the drink turns deep red

- Strain into a glass

- Garnish with orange peel and serve

Do you enjoy terrorising muggles? Are you evil to your very core? And do you treat others with utter contempt? If so, then this is surely the drink for you. All hail the Dark Lord!

*Glass: Old Fashioned*

- 3 parts whisky
- ½ part sugar syrup
- Large dash of Grenadine
- 1 part lime juice
- Orange peel
- Ice

# Viktor Krum

## Wronski Feint

It is best to use clear Tequila for this cocktail although it will taste just as good with any. A very refreshing drink with an unusual twang — that'll be the basil.

*Glass: Rocks*

- 2 parts tequila
- 4 parts soda water
- ½ part lime juice
- Mint leaves
- Basil
- Teaspoon of sugar
- Lime wedges
- Ice

→ Add the sugar, a little basil, mint leaves and lime juice to a glass

→ Crush and muddle then add tequila and stir

→ Fill the glass with soda

→ Garnish with lime wedges and serve

15

# Sybill Trelawney
## Crystal Ball

Stare deeply into this drink and it is said that those with 'the gift' can tell the future. No doubt it involves some awful and tragic event when read by certain people...

→ Put plenty of ice into a cocktail shaker

→ Pour in the vodka and coffee liqueur

→ Ready a glass half full of ice

→ Strain the shaker contents into the glass

→ Gently layer on the cream

→ Garnish with a cocktail cherry

→ Serve

Glass: Rocks

- 2½ parts vodka
- 1 part coffee liqueur
- 1½ parts single cream
- Cocktail cherry
- Ice

16

# Gilderoy Lockhart
## Mint Julep

The only thing Gilderoy Lockhart wouldn't like about this drink is that it isn't named after him! Great for drinking whilst signing autographs though...

- 3 parts bourbon
- ½ part water
- 1 tsp sugar
- A few mint leaves
- Crushed ice

→ Add the sugar and mint leaves to the glass

→ Add the water, then crush the mint leaves

→ Fill the glass ¾ full with crushed ice

→ Pour in the bourbon

→ Stir, garnish with a mint leaf or two

→ Serve

17

# Ron Weasley
## Fizzing Whizzbee

Ron's not exactly a master of potions, so he needs a drink that tastes great but is pretty easy to make. And this is it! The taste can vary greatly depending on the type of rum used...

* 2 parts Amaretto
* 3 parts spiced rum
* Cola to fill
* Ice

➤ Fill the glass half full with ice

➤ Add in the Amaretto and rum

➤ Fill with cola and stir

➤ Serve

*Glass: Large Rocks*

# Hagrid

## Rusty Nail

The recipe below is for a Hagrid-sized portion. Non-giants may wish to reduce the amount of each ingredient to a more sensible level for humans. The traditional name of this cocktail is actually 'Rusty Nail', although the twist of lemon peel is a non-standard addition.

- ◆ 20 parts whisky
- ◆ 20 parts Drambuie
- ◆ Lemon peel
- ◆ Ice

*Glass: Old Fashioned*

- ➤ Drop a kilo or so of ice into a large glass
- ➤ Add in the whisky and Drambuie
- ➤ Stir with a ladle
- ➤ Garnish with lemon peel
- ➤ Serve

19

# Barty Crouch Senior

## Meticulous Ministry Mixer

As head of the Department of Magical Law Enforcement, Mr Crouch would kindly request you measure the ingredients exactly so as to ensure a fully legally compliant drink...

- ➤ Fill the glass ¾ full with ice
- ➤ Pour in the gin and Triple Sec
- ➤ Stir well
- ➤ Add the lemon (for the discerning drinker to squeeze to taste)
- ➤ Serve

*Glass: Old Fashioned*

- ◆ 2 parts gin
- ◆ ½ part Triple Sec
- ◆ Lemon slice
- ◆ Ice

# Igor Karkaroff
## Black Russian

The only choice for Karkaroff is surely the classic black Russian (although the lemon is a modern addition). Perfect for warming the belly on a cold night in Durmstrang...

- 1 part coffee liqueur
- 1 ½ parts vodka
- Slice of lemon
- Ice

- Fill the glass half full with ice
- Pour the vodka slowly over the ice
- Add the coffee liquer (faster than the vodka) but don't stir
- Garnish with lemon slice
- Serve

*Glass: Rocks*

21

# Dobby

## Dobby's Downer

This drink is pleasant enough, but you wouldn't want to spend an entire evening with it — therefore best dealt with in small doses. After drinking you have to say "Harry Potter" in Dobby's voice.

*Glass: Shot*

- 1 part vodka
- 1 part Triple Sec
- 1 part lime juice
- Ice

→ Put some ice into a cocktail shaker

→ Add in the vodka, Triple Sec and lime juice

→ Shake well

→ Strain into a shot glass

→ Down in one

# Fenrir Greyback

## Greyback's Lethal Bite

One of the best-looking shooters you can make, this is a great drink for parties held on a full moon. Of course, you have to howl loudly after downing it...

*Glass: Shot*

- ½ part Baileys
- 1 part peach schnapps
- A few drops of Grenadine

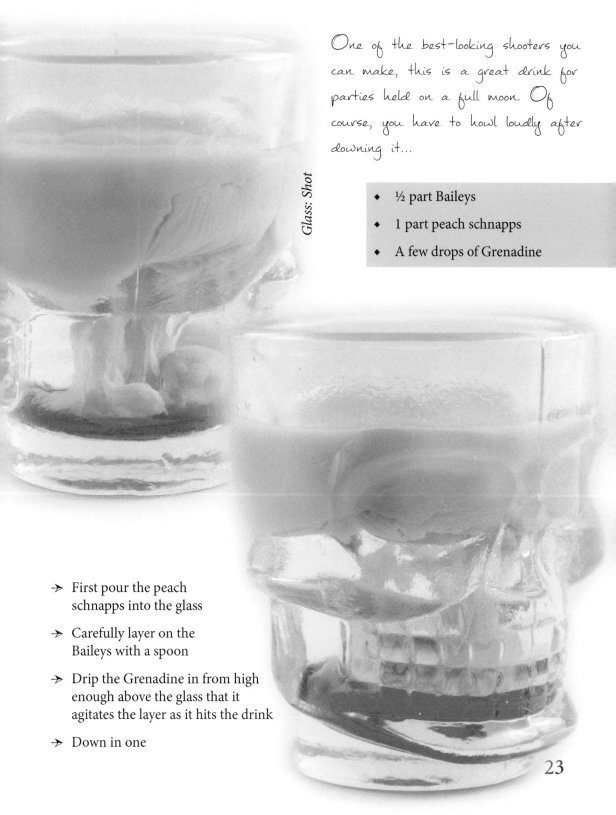

- ➤ First pour the peach schnapps into the glass
- ➤ Carefully layer on the Baileys with a spoon
- ➤ Drip the Grenadine in from high enough above the glass that it agitates the layer as it hits the drink
- ➤ Down in one

23

# Draco Malfoy

## Draco's Dark Arts

*The perfect way to practice your layering skills, this little shooter looks like a black-robed Malfoy. Much more pleasing than its Hogwarts counterpart though...*

- 1 part coffee liqueur
- 1 part Baileys

→ Pour in the coffee liqueur (don't let any touch the sides)

→ Carefully layer on the Baileys using a spoon to slow the pouring speed

→ Down in one

*Glass: Shot*

24

# Mad-Eye Moody
## The Auror

With just a wave of his wand, Mad-Eye can conjure up one of these quite easily. You, on the other hand, will just have to practice. Layering like this isn't <u>too</u> hard when you've done it a few times...

*Glass: Shot*

- ½ part vodka
- ½ part Blue Curacao
- ½ part Grenadine

➔ First carefully pour in the Grenadine

➔ Then, using a spoon, layer on the Curacao and next the vodka

➔ Fire off a few random curses

➔ Down in one

# Fred & George Weasley
## Weasley's Wizard Wheeze

This is the kind of shooter you make for someone else. You must tell the drinker to 'swish' the contents around in their mouth before swallowing — the 'joke' being that it curdles in the process, making the overall experience rather unpleasant. Hilarious.

*Glass: Shot*

- ◆ 1 part Baileys
- ◆ ½ part lime juice

➤ Pour the Baileys into a shot glass

➤ Carefully layer the lime juice on top

➤ Swirl the drink around your mouth a few times before swallowing

➤ Laugh heartily

26

# Nymphadora Tonks
# Metamorphmagus

Although traditionally called a 'cockroach', in the Harry Potter universe this cocktail is known as a Metamorphmagus because after downing it, your face will contort into all kinds of unusual positions you didn't realise it could go...

Glass: Shot

- ◆  1 ½ parts gold tequila
- ◆  1 part coffee liqueur

➤ Pour the coffee liqueur into a shot glass

➤ Gently layer the tequila on top

➤ If you're brave, light the tequila (and wait until the flame goes out)

➤ Down in one

# Molly Weasley
## Mollywobbles

A very sweet combination, the Mollywobbles is another shot that is just perfect for practising your layering skills. There's nothing in particular that links it with Molly herself, but the name is so good that it had to be used...

- ◆ 1 part Grenadine
- ◆ 1 part peach schnapps

➤ First carefully pour the Grenadine into a shot glass

➤ Then gently layer on the schnapps

➤ Down in one

# Crabbe & Goyle
## Scab & Boil

The idea here is to knock back the first drink ((Crabbe's 'Scab') and then straight afterwards down the second (Goyle's 'Boil'). They're actually not quite as foul as the names would suggest...

Glass: Shot

**Scab:**
- ◆ 1 part Sambuca
- ◆ 1 part Baileys

**Boil:**
- ◆ 1 part Sambuca
- ◆ 1 part whiskey

Scab:

➤ Half-fill the shot glass with Sambuca, then carefully layer on the Baileys

Boil:

➤ Mix the Sambuca and whiskey in a cocktail shaker and fill the shot glass to the brim.

# Horace Slughorn

## Poisonous Punch

The pineapple in this cocktail may not be crystallised, but it'll do for Slughorn. After one or two of these he'll regale you with stories of various witches and wizards in positions of power to whom he still sends the occasional owl, then sing a sad song about a wizard called Odo...

*Glass: Wine*

- 2 parts Midori
- 2 parts Malibu
- 4 parts pineapple juice
- Ice

→ Fill a cocktail shaker with ice

→ Add the ingredients and shake well

→ Strain into a glass and serve

# Ginny Weasley

## Tequila Sunrise

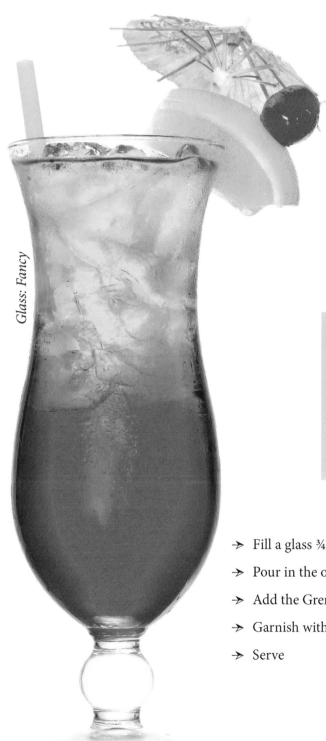

This is a great-looking cocktail that isn't too hard to make. If you hold a cocktail party, this is sure to be one of the most commonly requested drinks, so it is well worth learning how to make one...

Glass: Fancy

- 2 parts tequila
- 1 part Grenadine
- 4 parts orange juice
- Slice of orange
- Cocktail cherry
- Ice

→ Fill a glass ¾ full of ice
→ Pour in the orange juice and tequila and stir
→ Add the Grenadine slowly
→ Garnish with the orange slice and cherry
→ Serve

# Fleur Delacour

## Cosmopolitan

We're pretty sure that this is the perfect drink for Fleur. Classy it may be — perhaps even a little snobbish — but pretty tasty nonetheless.

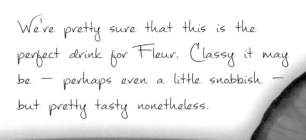

- ½ to ¾ parts Cointreau
- 2 parts vodka
- ½ part lime juice
- 2 parts cranberry juice
- Slice of lime
- Dash of lemon juice
- Ice

Glass: Martini

- → Add ice to a cocktail shaker
- → Add the vodka, Cointreau, Lime juice and cranberry juice
- → Squirt in a small dash of lemon juice
- → Shake well
- → Strain into the Martini glass
- → Garnish with the slice of lime
- → Serve

32

# Cedric Diggory

# Dry Martini

Suave and sophisticated, this drink is the perfect match for Cedric. A real martini like this is made with gin and not vodka.

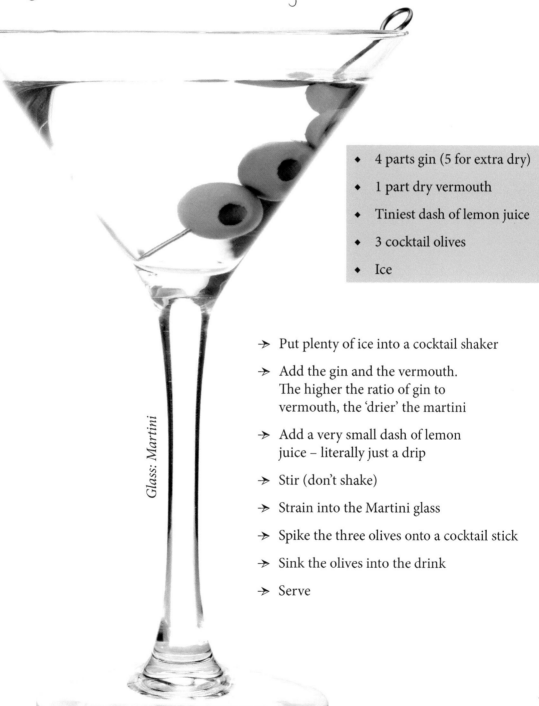

*Glass: Martini*

- ◆ 4 parts gin (5 for extra dry)
- ◆ 1 part dry vermouth
- ◆ Tiniest dash of lemon juice
- ◆ 3 cocktail olives
- ◆ Ice

➤ Put plenty of ice into a cocktail shaker

➤ Add the gin and the vermouth. The higher the ratio of gin to vermouth, the 'drier' the martini

➤ Add a very small dash of lemon juice – literally just a drip

➤ Stir (don't shake)

➤ Strain into the Martini glass

➤ Spike the three olives onto a cocktail stick

➤ Sink the olives into the drink

➤ Serve

33

# Hermione Granger
## Bellini

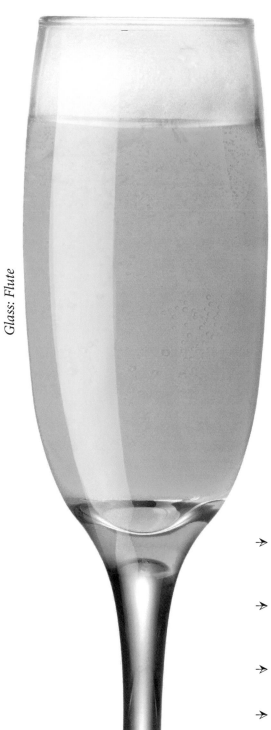

*Glass: Flute*

You might have to search around for peach juice (or purée) but like a rare book from deep within the library's restricted section, it is worth seeking out so you can make this drink!

- ◆ 4 parts champagne (or other sparkling white wine)
- ◆ 2 parts peach juice (or puree for a thicker drink)
- ◆ Twist of orange peel

➤ Make sure your champagne and juice are already chilled

➤ Pour the juice and champagne into the glass and stir gently

➤ Garnish with orange peel

➤ Serve

34

# Luna Lovegood

# Gulping Plimpy

It might not have the most appealing name, but surely it's better than "Crumple-Horned Snorkack" or "Umgubular Slashkilter". Too many of these and you'll think you're wearing spectrespecs though...

*Glass: Martini*

- ◆ 2 parts gin
- ◆ 1 part brandy
- ◆ ½ part lemon juice
- ◆ A dash or two of Grenadine
- ◆ Ice

➤ Add ice to your shaker

➤ Pour in the gin, brandy, Grenadine and lemon juice then shake well

➤ Strain and serve

# Remus Lupin
## Lupin's Lush Liqour

*This cocktail's traditional name is 'Amaretto Sour', and although it is very easy to make, it is hard to perfect: you may need practice to find <u>exactly</u> the right amount of lemon juice!*

- ◆ 2 parts Amaretto
- ◆ 1 part lemon juice
- ◆ Sugar
- ◆ Cocktail cherry
- ◆ Ice

*Glass: Martini*

- ↣ Fill a cocktail shaker with ice
- ↣ Add in the Amaretto and lemon juice
- ↣ Shake well
- ↣ Coat the rim of the glass with sugar
- ↣ Pour the drink carefully into the glass
- ↣ Drop in a cocktail cherry
- ↣ Serve

36

# Cornelius Fudge
# Chocolatini

It would have been great to have made this into a fudgetini, however the chocolate version is much more popular (and the ingredients easier to source!) The key here is presentation: it should look more like a dessert than an actual drink...

*Glass: Martini*

- 1½ part Baileys
- 1 part vodka
- ½ parts Crème de Cacao
- Chocolate shavings
- Cocoa powder
- Ice

→ Fill a cocktail shaker with ice

→ Pour in the Crème, vodka and Baileys and shake well

→ Slightly wet the rim of the glass and dip it in cocoa powder

→ Shake the liquids well and strain into the glass

→ Throw on a few shavings of chocolate

→ Serve

# Xenophilius Lovegood

# Quibbler

When you're planning on searching for the Deathly Hallows whilst simultaneously publishing a magazine that reveals the conspiracies no-one else will even mention, it surely helps to have a drink that will increase your brain power. Sadly, this isn't it — what you <u>really</u> need is Baruffio's Brain Elixir...

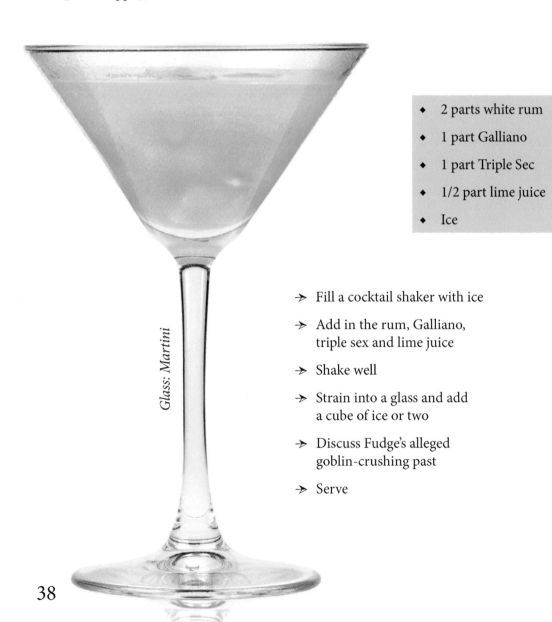

*Glass: Martini*

- ◆ 2 parts white rum
- ◆ 1 part Galliano
- ◆ 1 part Triple Sec
- ◆ 1/2 part lime juice
- ◆ Ice

➤ Fill a cocktail shaker with ice

➤ Add in the rum, Galliano, triple sex and lime juice

➤ Shake well

➤ Strain into a glass and add a cube of ice or two

➤ Discuss Fudge's alleged goblin-crushing past

➤ Serve

# Neville Longbottom
# Mimbulus Mimbletonia

Even Neville should be able to make this cocktail, despite the difficulty he has with potions — well, as long as Snape isn't standing over his shoulder watching him mix the ingredients that is...

→ Fill a cocktail shaker with ice

→ Add in the Midori, Cointreau and lemon juice

→ Shake well

→ Strain into a glass and drop in the cherry

→ Serve

*Glass: Martini*

- ◆ 2 parts Midori
- ◆ 2 parts Cointreau
- ◆ 1 part lemon juice
- ◆ Cocktail cherry
- ◆ Ice

# Rita Skeeter
# Marga-Rita

This is another one of those cocktails that is such a classic that you really should learn how to make a good one. Experts usually add in a touch more Cointreau and a little less lime juice than a perfect 50/50 split as listed here...

- ◆ 2 parts tequila
- ◆ 1 part Cointreau
- ◆ 1 part lime juice
- ◆ Slice of lime
- ◆ Salt
- ◆ Ice

➜ Fill a cocktail shaker with ice

➜ Add in the tequila, Cointreau and lime juice

➜ Shake well

➜ Wet the rim of a glass and dip in salt

➜ Strain the shaker into the glass

➜ Garnish with lime wedge

➜ Serve

*Glass: Martini*

# Severus Snape

# Overflowing Cauldron

This cocktail certainly wouldn't look out of place bubbling away in a cauldron in Snape's dungeon classroom, although thankfully you don't need his exquisite potion skills to make one of these. The ingredients might not strictly be every day bottles, but they're worth investing in for this great drink...

- ➤ Fill a cocktail shaker with ice

- ➤ Add in the two Crèmes and the cream and shake well

- ➤ Wet the rim of a glass and dip in cocoa powder

- ➤ Strain the cocktail into the glass

- ➤ Serve

*Glass: Martini*

- ◆ 2 parts Crème de Cacao
- ◆ 2 parts Crème de Menthe
- ◆ 2 parts single cream
- ◆ Cocoa Powder
- ◆ Ice

41

# Cho Chang

## Cho's Chocolate Crush

This cocktail most likely takes the record for having more calories than any other in this book. It is a sweet-lover's delight. Be careful though, its amazing taste masks just how strong it is...

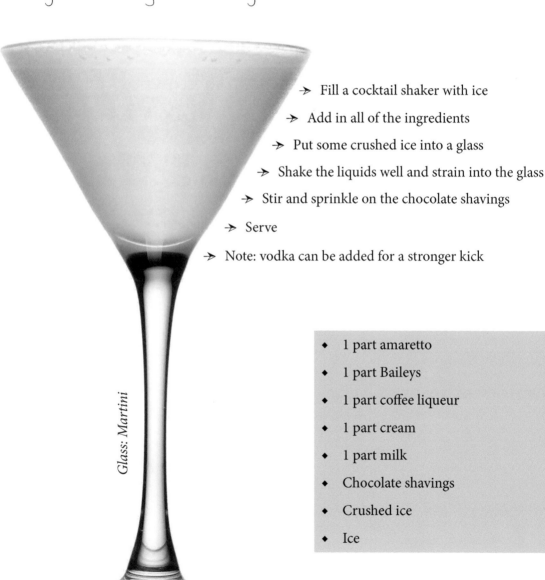

Glass: Martini

➤ Fill a cocktail shaker with ice

➤ Add in all of the ingredients

➤ Put some crushed ice into a glass

➤ Shake the liquids well and strain into the glass

➤ Stir and sprinkle on the chocolate shavings

➤ Serve

➤ Note: vodka can be added for a stronger kick

- 1 part amaretto
- 1 part Baileys
- 1 part coffee liqueur
- 1 part cream
- 1 part milk
- Chocolate shavings
- Crushed ice
- Ice

# Delores Umbridge
# Educational Decree No. 43

You can just imagine Umbridge sipping daintily at one of these whilst watching Harry write his lines. Traditionally known as a 'pink gin', this is a drink with plenty of history...

Glass: Martini

- ◆ 2 parts gin
- ◆ 1 dash angostura bitters
- ◆ Lime wedge
- ◆ Ice

➤ Fill a cocktail shaker with ice

➤ Add in the gin and angostura

➤ Shake until enough ice has melted to fill the glass

➤ Strain and garnish with lime

➤ Serve

# Madame Maxine

## French Kiss

Oh, c'est tres belle Madame!
Her horses might drink only
the finest single malt whisky,
but this is the kind of cocktail
Madame Maxine prefers. Just
follow the instructions and voila!

- 2 parts tequila
- 1 part black raspberry liqueur
- 1 part white Crème de Cacao
- 1 part single cream
- Ice

*Glass: Martini*

→ Put some ice into a cocktail shaker

→ Add in the tequila, liqueur and Crème de Cacao

→ Pour in the cream then shake well

→ Strain and serve

44

# Bellatrix Lestrange

## Horcrux

- → Fill a cocktail shaker with ice
- → Add in the rum, sugar syrup and lemon juice
- → Shake well then strain into a glass
- → Add soda to fill
- → Garnish with lemon slices and lemon peel
- → Serve (the Dark Lord)

*Glass: Large Rocks*

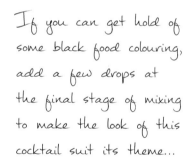

*If you can get hold of some black food colouring, add a few drops at the final stage of mixing to make the look of this cocktail suit its theme...*

- ◆ 2 parts white rum
- ◆ 1 part sugar syrup
- ◆ 1 part lemon juice
- ◆ Soda
- ◆ Lemon slice
- ◆ Lemon peel
- ◆ Ice

# Garrick Ollivander
## Wobbly Wand

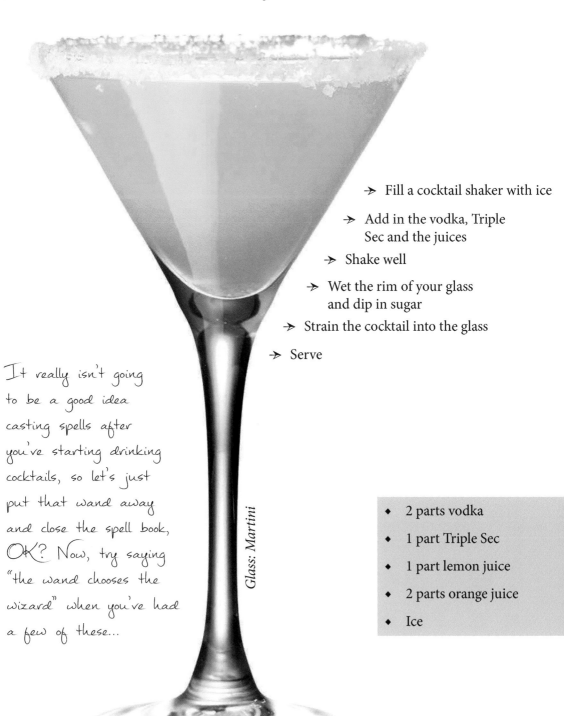

→ Fill a cocktail shaker with ice

→ Add in the vodka, Triple Sec and the juices

→ Shake well

→ Wet the rim of your glass and dip in sugar

→ Strain the cocktail into the glass

→ Serve

It really isn't going to be a good idea casting spells after you've starting drinking cocktails, so let's just put that wand away and close the spell book, OK? Now, try saying "the wand chooses the wizard" when you've had a few of these...

*Glass: Martini*

- ◆ 2 parts vodka
- ◆ 1 part Triple Sec
- ◆ 1 part lemon juice
- ◆ 2 parts orange juice
- ◆ Ice

# Seamus Finnigan
## Irish Coffee

Well this shouldn't be much of a surprise. Not necessarily a party cocktail, more one for later on in the evening when the _real_ conversation starts...

- → Fill the glass ¾ full with coffee

- → Add in the sugar and stir.

- → Pour in the whisky and stir again

- → Top the drink off with whipped cream and add a light dusting of sprinkles to your guest's choosing

- → Serve

_Glass: Handled_

- ◆ Hot coffee
- ◆ 1 shot of whisky
- ◆ 1 spoonful brown sugar
- ◆ Whipped cream
- ◆ Sprinkles of chocolate or nuts

# Non-Alcoholic Drinks

# The Creevey Brothers
# Common Room Cordial

If you don't give the Creeveys their own drink, you just know they're going to pester you for the rest of the evening. Here's one for them — although be careful, the sugar content might make them a little hyperactive...

*Glass: Collins*

- ◆ 1 part lime cordial
- ◆ 7 parts orange juice
- ◆ ½ part Grenadine
- ◆ Orange slice
- ◆ Ice

↠ Fill the glass ¾ full with ice

↠ Add in the orange juice and lime cordial then stir

↠ Pour in the grenadine

↠ Drop in an orange slice or two

↠ Serve

# Dudley Dursley

## Big D

This cocktail is better known as a Shirley Temple, named after a cute little child actor from the 1930s. Just don't tell Big D or he might get a bit angry...

- ½ part lime juice
- 1 part Grenadine
- 1 part orange juice
- Ginger beer
- Lime slices
- Cocktail cherry
- Ice

→ Fill the glass ½ full with ice

→ Pour in the lime juice, Grenadine and orange juice

→ Add the ginger beer to fill whilst stirring

→ Garnish with lime slices and cherry

→ Serve

Glass: Collins

51

# Pomona Sprout

## Professor's Pineapple Pop

Depending on your taste you can add more or less soda water; some people enjoy this in a Collins glass with an extra dollop of honey and soda to fill...

*Glass: Martini*

- Add everything but the soda water to a blender
- Blend together then add soda and stir
- Strain into the glass
- Garnish with coconut slice
- Serve

- 1 teaspoon of sugar
- 1 tablespoon of honey
- 2 parts pineapple juice
- Soda water
- Coconut slice
- Ice

# The Patil Twins

## Nojito

This is a close as it gets to a full Mojito without the alcohol. Making a good Nojito will actually test your potions skills pretty well, so be prepared to practice...

*Glass: Collins*

- 1 part lemon juice
- ¾ part lime juice
- 1 part sugar syrup
- Lemonade
- 2 slices of cucumber
- Mint leaves
- Ice

→ Add the sugar syrup and mint leaves to a glass and crush

→ Finely chop the cucumber and add to the glass

→ Next add the ice, lemon and lime juice

→ Stir whilst adding lemonade and a couple more mint leaves

→ Serve

53

Thanks for reading this book — now why not create some cocktails of your own!

Archie X

CPSIA information can be obtained
at www.ICGtesting.com
Printed in the USA
LVIC06n0857191216
517887LV00011B/112

* 9 7 8 1 7 8 5 3 8 6 1 1 4 *